T0354655

Rendezvous

Rev. Michele Jackson Taylor

authorHOUSE®

AuthorHouse™
1663 Liberty Drive
Bloomington, IN 47403
www.authorhouse.com
Phone: 1 (800) 839-8640

Published by AuthorHouse 03/16/2018

ISBN: 978-1-5462-3158-5 (sc)
ISBN: 978-1-5462-3156-1 (hc)
ISBN: 978-1-5462-3157-8 (e)

Library of Congress Control Number: 2018902743

Print information available on the last page.

King James Version (KJV)
Scriptures were taken from The King James Version of The Bible - Public Domain.

Rendezvous is dedicated to the victorious women and men who have overcome emotional, physical, mental and spiritual challenges, and those who are still journeying through.

Our God is "able to do exceeding abundantly above all that we ask or think, according to the power that worketh in us" (Ephesians 3:20, KJV).

In Loving Memory

Edna Piccola-Lewis
Supervisor of Women,
Third Ecclesiastical Jurisdiction, Eastern New York
Resting in the Lord - September 2, 2017

I cherish our conversations about releasing the books that the Holy Spirit inspired us to write to lift, build and encourage God's people. Your endearing smile is forever embedded in my heart.

ACKNOWLEDGEMENTS

All praises to God for whispering creative thoughts into my ears, and the flow of the Holy Spirit that influenced me to pen what I heard.

My heart declares a very special *"thank you"* to some wonderful behind-the-scenes loved ones. I feel extremely blessed.

Chenelle Nixon, my friend, mentee and daughter in Christ: You were the first to hear the concept and story line of **Rendezvous**. You enthusiastically gave the thumbs-up and high-five response that ignited the start of another MJT (Michele Jackson Taylor) project.

L.G. Williams (Viceroy Entertainment): Your spiritual insight about the bigger picture of God's plan for the finished work pushed me to get the job done.

Linda Boyce, my big sister: You're the voice of wisdom and sound judgment. You listened to the first read while we enjoyed a balcony view of the tropical grounds and tranquil blue waters of Turks & Caicos—good times.

My family: Natural, spiritual and extended. Keeping it real, your unconditional love keeps me balanced. Hugs all around!

Rev. Tina Baker: Your courage to share your own journey in order to help others reminded me that our stories are not our own. They must be shared so that others can be encouraged and inspired to press on.

Marilyn A. Hunte (Bestie): My beloved sister and friend. You've taught me so much about celebrating life in these past few years alone, never mind the other 30+ years of our friendship. I celebrate you.

The *Sisterhood of the Brooklyn Community Church:* Celebrating Women's Day 2017 with you was a privilege, joy, uplift to my spirit and confirmation to release **Rendezvous**. To God be the glory.

FOREWORD

The unforgettable moment when a person accepts Jesus into their life is unique to one's own experience, yet the results are the same for all. *Rendezvous* skillfully articulates the peaceful joy that rests upon the life of those who encounter the Savior. Author Rev. Michele Jackson Taylor has delivered a book full of healing and recovery. The genius of using testimonies as the foundation of this piece makes it relatable to all who read it. Addressing hard-hitting topics that many face, but do not openly discuss, this work evokes the courage to confront, the strength to endure, and assurance that Jesus is the answer. *Rendezvous* will intrigue, inspire and ignite the ability to completely trust in God's plan for your life. I have no doubt that this book will expand your thinking and bless your life.

Pastor Tina Baker,
Bethsalem Baptist Church
Author: "Feeling Trapped? There is a Way Out,"
"Become Who You Are Born to Be," and "Exiting the Waiting Room"
Hempstead, NY

CHAPTER 1

Welcome

"Welcome! It's standing-room only."

A silver-haired usher adorned in an ankle-length white skirt and long-sleeved purple blouse greeted me as I walked through the double-door entrance of The Redeemer Church—a small store-front in Brooklyn that accommodates all of seventy-five people. I felt welcomed by her inviting smile.

A sea of purple and white dresses, skirts and blouses, lap scarves, and purple bow ties caught my attention. Music bounced off the walls filling the building with sounds of spirited rhythms. A five-member choir lifted their voices to the melody of "Praise is What I Do." Hands waving in the air, thunderous claps, and cries of praise echoed as sisters worshipped in the pews and aisles, and brothers surveyed like protective soldiers.

"I haven't seen this many folk on a Second Sunday afternoon in a long time," the usher proclaimed.

"Then again, Women's Day always brings out a large crowd. Everyone wants to celebrate the wonderful achievements of the 'Ladies in the House.' They worked so hard to make it a great event."

"Everyone looks lovely," I observed. "So this is Women's Day?"

"It sure is, son. We're so happy you could join us. Let me see if I can find a seat for you." She looked around, walked to the front of the building and returned. "Not an empty seat in the house. Praise our God!" She said with delight.

"I'm okay to stand here in the back, if it's alright."

"Of course it is." She continued, "This is a special day."

"How so?" I asked.

"It's a celebration of something wonderful! Something magnificent! Something only God could do. I've seen miracles right here! You know, mothers see everything." Her eyes pierced mine as though she was looking right through me.

I had no idea what she was talking about, but her enthusiasm drew me in. I wanted to know what made this year's celebration more special than any other—why this refined elderly woman smiled so radiantly, as if she was the keeper of a big secret.

I waited patiently hoping a seat would become available; but none did, and there was no room in the aisle for another folding chair.

"If you get tired of standing, you can watch the service downstairs in the Overflow Room. At least you can sit comfortably."

"That sounds good right about now," I admitted.

"Come on, son. Follow me."

So I did. Another usher quickly moved into her spot as we exited the sanctuary and descended a narrow staircase leading to the basement. No sooner than we entered a quaint dining room with a wide-screen television did she begin to point at the screen.

"Now, I've seen these sisters worshipping Sunday after Sunday. I tell you, they are truly one in the spirit. The experiences that separated their worlds are the very ones that brought them together in celebration today."

I'm sure I had a puzzled look on my face that said, "Huh?"

"Each one of these sisters' lives was miraculously changed. You see, their testimonies are quite unique. That's why they're praising God like there's no tomorrow."

"They definitely seem happy," I commented. "What's the deal?"

"Well, what you're looking at is a *rendezvous* with the Holy Spirit. Glory!" she bellowed and did a two-step dance with her hand on her hip. "Like the words of this song, praise is what we do!"

She pointed to several women who began to dance as the tempo of the music quickened. "That's Glenda, Ramona, Celeste, Jasmine, Mother Sharmaine and Melody."

"And you? What's your name?" I finally asked.

"Oh mercy! Where are my manners? I'm Mother Jean. Most folk just call me, Mother."

"It's nice to meet you, Mother Jean. I'm Russell." She shook my hand firmly and took a seat opposite me at a long table facing the screen. So began a litany of amazing testimonies that blew me away.

CHAPTER 2

Glenda

(A Walking Miracle)

ço

"Nineteen, single, alone and distraught—that's how Glenda described herself. She was recuperating from an accident that left her wheelchair-bound. Tall, slender, creamy complexion, a waistline to die for, golden hair—and not one of those weaves, either. It's all hers—natural. To me, she looks a lot like Mariah Carey. I know she's bi-racial, but she never did tell me the blend."

"*Mother,*" she'd say. "*The United Nations lives inside of me. I come from a mixed bag. One day, God put His hand in that bag, and this is what He pulled out—me.*"

"Oh, we'd laugh and laugh till our sides ached. Well, whatever was in that bag, God pulled out a beautiful girl that grew into an even more beautiful woman. She was a model, you know. That's right—landed her first job posing for a children's clothing store when she was seven. Said she did a lot of catalogue print until she was sixteen. That's when her big break came…and her sudden tragedy."

"*Why me?*" she asked. "*Why did God do this to me?*"

"Now, I didn't have the answer. Who can know the mind of God? All I could tell her was that God knew the reason. He knew what she'd have to face and how she'd handle herself in the process."

"What happened?" I asked.

5

"The way Glenda tells it, the producer made her climb some boulders at the base of a waterfall in Mexico for a photo shoot. That hard water cascading on top of her, and those slippery rocks—she didn't stand a chance. *'These things happen all the time.'* That's what the producer told her. Of course, her parents sued the agency, but she never talks about the results. It's funny, though. Every year there's an anonymous donation to the Missions Fund. A lot of people in the community are helped by that donation."

"You think it's Glenda?"

"I do! We all do, but no one says a word. Only the accountant knows for sure."

"So how did she come to The Redeemer Church?"

"It was New Year's Eve. The snow had come down so hard and furious, it's amazing anyone came to church that night. A man rolled the wheelchair to the front of the sanctuary. This thin, pale young lady sat crumpled—her torso slouched over, and her legs looked stiff on the footrest. I can remember the sadness on her face. Helplessness daunted her demeanor. Yet, there seemed to be a glimmer of hope in her eyes. She told her story and burst into tears. I'm paraphrasing, but basically this is what she revealed to the congregation."

"The doctors said I would never walk again. After multiple surgeries and physical therapy, I'm still in this chair. Nineteen years of age, and I'm still in this chair. I'm angry, and I'm angry at God. Why did He do this to me? I'm tired, and I feel dead inside, but I want to live. I want to walk again. I don't want to be bound to this chair for the rest of my life. So I can't give up. If there's a God, then He will heal me. If God heals me, I will walk for Him. I will walk for Jesus. So He's going to heal me. He has to."

"I tell you, with all the celebrating going on to bring in the New

Year, this weeping-willow made time stand still." Mother paused and took a deep breath.

"Then what happened?" I was enthralled. I had to know the rest of the story.

"Well, Pastor called out, *'I need seven mothers to come down here right now. Not just church mothers—mothers who believe God for this daughter. Mothers who know God can heal **her** because He healed you.'*

"They came—one by one—seven women of all different races, ages, shapes and sizes. Pastor said, *'We're going to pray for this daughter. God is going to heal her. If you have faith the size of a grain of a mustard seed, you can move mountains. Does anybody in here have mustard seed faith tonight? Does anyone believe that God will heal this young lady? Say 'Amen' if you believe.'*

I tell you, the whole church shouted, *'Amen.' 'Hallelujah'* filled the sanctuary. Pastor laid hands on Glenda, and those mothers prayed like thunder rolling through the atmosphere. The praises went up like Jesus had just cracked the sky and stepped down from Glory right on that altar. Oh, I tell you, the sight of it all was something to behold.

Glenda cried and cried and cried. Her arms stretched towards the heavens as if God Himself had beckoned her to come forth. She gripped that chair, braced herself and lifted her body. She grabbed one of those mothers' hands, stood up out of that wheelchair and took a step. Tears and all, she took another step. Then one more step and another and another.

I don't think she even noticed the saints praising God. I tell you, the visitors got an eyeful that night. Ten people gave their lives to Christ. That's right—10 souls were saved because of that young lady right there taking those few short steps."

"That had to be something to see!" I declared.

"It sure was. When she went to the doctor two months later

7

walking with a mere limp, they declared that it was a medical phenomenon. They couldn't believe what they saw. You know what she told them?"

"What?"

"She said, *'I called on Doctor Jesus, and He healed me.'* The physical therapist—a Believer—contended that her faith made her whole and gave her the strength she needed to get out of that wheelchair because her body had already healed.

I'm not a doctor, so I can't speak about those things—whether or not the body had already healed itself. What I do know is that more than a year and a half has come and gone since that glorious miracle on New Year's Eve. Now look at her dance!"

"What a miracle," I concurred.

The Praise Team sang on not knowing the timeliness of their words at the conclusion of Mother Jean's story. *"Praise is what I doooooo-oooo. It's what I do."*

CHAPTER 3

Ramona

(Chocolate Cake)

❧

"This sister here," Mother pointed to a pretty Latina woman getting her dance on in the third pew.

"What's her story?" I asked. Mother gave me a look as if to say—"this is a good one."

"Ramona is from DR—the Dominican Republic—La Republica Dominicana. I remember the day she received salvation. It's funny how things slip your mind, and then they come back like it happened yesterday.

Everything about that Friday was crazy. A Nor'easter piled two feet of white fluff on the city. 'Deserted' best describes the streets. With the exception of a few people bundled up in bubble coats walking briskly to their destinations, not a creature was stirring—to coin a phrase from that ole Christmas Carol. It was so bad that mass transportation was brought to a halt. Not one bus moved since mid-morning, and elevated trains remained in storage underground.

Now that I recall, there were a few power outages, too, because the high winds blew down tree branches onto power lines. The best thing to do was to stay home and bake. I'm telling on myself," she laughed. "I figured I'd bake a few cakes and carry one to the senior center down the block, one to the day care across the street if it opened, and keep

9

one for myself. Not only did I bake three cakes, I rolled out a few dozen chocolate chip and oatmeal raisin cookies, too. Then I figured I might as well make dinner. Once I started, I didn't stop until there was a spread of food on the table like Thanksgiving—roasted chicken, real mashed potatoes with sautéed onions and mushrooms, fresh greens and cornbread."

"Mother, you're making me hungry." I licked my lips imagining the taste of succulent collard greens.

"Well, it must have been the aroma of all that food that drew Ramona to my front door. It was only around 4:30, but darkness had fallen. Three times that buzzer rang. I said to myself, '*who on earth is leaning on my bell?*' When I opened the door, there she was."

"*Hola. Su baño por favor. I need to use the bathroom, please.*"

"Her face was reddish purple, and she was shivering. What was I supposed to do, let her stand there freezing?"

"Of course not." I declared.

"Exactly," she continued the dialogue. "*Good Lord. Come in here, child. The bathroom's this way.*"

"*Thank you.*"

"She closed the door behind her so fast that I didn't get to tell her where to find the light switch. As soon as she came out, I could see the expression of relief. Then she hugged me, and I knew—a change was about to happen. I could feel the warmth of her spirit."

"*Thank you, thank you.*"

"*Where'd you come from? What happened?*"

"*The buses stopped, and I walked for hours. I could no longer hold myself. If I let go, surely it would freeze.*"

"Her infectious laugh made me laugh so hard, I had to...well, anyway. A beautiful smile came over her face, and she hugged me again. I asked her where she was going, and she told me, 'Avenue H.'

"*Oh honey, that's a long way from here. At least an hour walk in the snow. You'd better rest yourself and get your strength. Are you hungry?' I asked her.*"

"*Yes, thank you. Your cake smells good.*"

"*Child, you need some warm food in your belly—then cake. What's your name?*"

"*Ramona. Ramona Iglesia Seraphin,*" she told me.

"*That's a pretty name. Doesn't 'Iglesia' mean church?*"

"*Si'. Mi madre es muy religiosa. Pero me, no.*"

"*I don't understand. My Spanish is little.*"

"*My mother is very religious, but not me.*"

"We ate and talked and talked and ate. She told me that she worked on the other side of Myrtle Avenue and had to walk home when the buses stopped running. People were walking, so she walked, too. She said the roads were pretty bad, and cars were sliding into each other and into parked cars. Even emergency vehicles were having trouble getting around. Said she tried to use the bathroom in a few stores she saw along the way, but they were closed, and she had to stop somewhere. Of all things, the smell of cake drew her to my door."

"*Your food is good! Bueno! And your home is so warm, but I must go now.*"

"I saw her look over at that chocolate cake, so I sliced several pieces and placed the plate in front of her. Her eyes lit up like Christmas," Mother continued.

"*Chocolate! My favorite.*"

Mother leaned in and gave me a stern look. "There was no way I would let her back out in that cold. So I said, '*Tell me your story. Why you don't have religion?*"

"*Mi madre—my mother went to the cathedral all the time. She prayed to St. Mary always with rosary beads in her hands. She lit candles and gave to the poor. I said, 'madre', why do you give to the poor when we are poor, too? She said we have rice, and they don't."*

"I told her that her mother sounded like a very generous person. Then she told me her mother died a few years ago, and she was still angry. She wanted to know why God let her mother die after all that praying she did. All I could say was that it had to have been hard on her, but God knew the answer."

"'Very hard,' she said. 'I watched her try to be strong when everyday she was in pain. Her smile wasn't real. Her God wasn't real."

"'God is real, child. He's very real.' I insisted."

"'Then why'd he let my mother die? I told him I wasn't ready for her to leave me. I told him I couldn't make it on my own without her. I told him that I didn't understand why he took my father when I was only three, and now he wanted her, too. How fair is that? How righteous is that? She worked many jobs to make money so we had rice. She gave to others even though we had little. She was a saint, and he took her away from me. She taught me to work—to clean houses so I could make money. I went to school to get a diploma, but she didn't live to see me graduate. Where is this God she prayed to? You tell me. Where is he?"

"'Right here, in your heart.' I told her, 'I know you're angry. I guess I would be too. But it seems to me that God took your mother because she was in pain. Maybe he didn't want her to suffer anymore. Maybe he knew that it was better for her to sleep, and that you would be alright. Your mother gave you what you need to live. She taught you skills and made sure you got an education.'

Son, I tell you, it broke my heart when she said, *'I dreamed to be somebody—to make mama proud. Now I just clean houses, and my dreams are dead. So where is this God?'*

'Right here,' I told her. 'Open your heart to him."

"Thanks, but no thanks. You were very kind to open your door to me, but now I must go."

Mother leaned back and smiled. "Well, the doorbell rang at just that moment." She got excited with each word. "I thought to myself, *'who could that possibly be in this weather?'* I opened the door, and guess who was standing there?"

"Who?" I impatiently asked.

"My pastor! I was too surprised. He said he was checking on the saints to see if we were alright or needed anything, and then he handed me two bags filled with groceries from the pantry.

'I'm doing just fine,' I told him. *'Cleaned the sidewalk this morning, cooked and baked a few cakes. You come on in here and have some dinner.'*

"You know I could never pass up your good cooking, Mother Jean."

"Pastor, there's someone I want you to meet. The young lady's about to leave, but God sent you right on time.'

"By the time Pastor finished telling Ramona about the goodness of God and how Christ died on the cross at Calvary to save her—I tell you, it was like the angels in heaven came and sat down on my sofa to listen in. Through tears, that young lady said yes to salvation. Then Pastor laid hands on her forehead and declared, *'En el nombre de Jesus Christo.'* It was a miracle before my own eyes. Now look at her—shouting for joy."

I couldn't help but smile as my eyes focused back to the television and saw Ramona dancing up a storm. "That's some testimony, Mother Jean."

"That's not all. The Lord opened a door for her to go to culinary school. Now, she's an assistant chef at an up-scale restaurant in Manhattan."

I found myself staring at the screen saying, "God is good."

Mother softly responded, "All the time."

CHAPTER 4

Celeste

(Spaghetti and Meat Sauce)

᳄

I Stood up and stretched my legs. The choir kept singing like there was no tomorrow. Surely, by now a seat was available in the sanctuary. Mother Jean excused herself and ascended up the narrow stairway to take a look. A few short minutes, and she returned.

"There was a seat, but a woman with a baby came. I guess you're stuck with me."

Two more people entered the Overflow Room. Mother Jean instructed them to join us at the table. "I was telling Brother Russell here about all these sisters you see dancing in the spirit." The couple smiled and kept talking among themselves. She wasn't fazed by their disinterest.

"This is Celeste," she pointed to a young lady that couldn't have been more than twenty-eight or twenty-nine. Her short, black curly hair rounded her slender face.

"Celeste cries a lot," Mother continued. "Every time I looked around, she was crying. And I mean real bucket tears—the kind of tears that make you want to cry, too. See what I mean? She's over there crying right now. But those are tears of joy—not pain."

Pain, as Celeste described it, was two black eyes, a wallop to the gut, bald spots from hair pulled out by the roots and purple bruises on her

15

back from '*that man*' pouncing her. 'Whipper' found a reason to knock the stew out of her just about every day.

Once he got mad at her because dinner wasn't on the table when he came home from work. Mind you, she worked, too. Do you know how difficult it is to work, make sure your five children are situated, homework done, and then put dinner on the table? Well, she tried her best, and usually succeeded; but if ever she missed a beat, she got the beat-down. One night, she had had enough. The way Celeste tells it, Whipper and a pile of spaghetti with meat sauce lay limp on the kitchen floor. Said she didn't know if the red liquid surrounding his body was sauce or blood. I reckon it was both. Everyone has a breaking point, you know."

"What happened?" I found myself staring at the screen wondering what this petite young woman waving her hands towards the ceiling in praise could have done.

"I heard she was stirring the pot when the two little ones ran to the door to greet their daddy. Whipper leaned down to kiss them, and then moved them aside before slamming his newspaper on the table in front of Celeste. He and Celeste got to arguing about something when a fist came across her jaw so hard she fell back against the stove and burnt her arm on that pot."

"Oh my God," I gasped at the thought of what I envisioned.

"I'm telling you, Celeste said she doubled over in pain even more when she saw the frightened faces of her babies. Before she could catch her balance, another punch propelled her against the wall. Then another one landed her to the floor. The kids were screaming and pulling on their daddy's legs to keep him from kicking their mama. He managed to get a few into her side and stomach before knocking one of them little ones across the room."

"How did she get away?" I needed to know!

"She didn't. She lay still in her own urine until he walked away. The kids found a hiding place in closets and under the bed. When Celeste finally picked herself up off the floor, the time had come. Said she'd cleaned herself up—and the floor too. Put the kids to bed, piled spaghetti on a plate and served her husband like nothing happened. No sooner than he sprawled out on the sofa watching football—half sleep, half woke and cussing under his breath—that sister right there," she pointed, "bruises and all—doused that man with the remains in that pot. Then she called the police, opened the front door and sat at the kitchen table.

Whipper whooped and hollered so loud, the neighbors came running in the door to see what happened. There he was on the floor curled up in a ball all drenched in pasta and sauce with skin peeling off his face and hands. Celeste confessed on the spot. *'Yeah, I did it, and I'd do it again.'* I think she was in a state of shock, though. Neighbors said she wouldn't let go of that pot."

"What about the children?"

"Temporary custody was given to Celeste's sister, and they had to go to therapy. They had no problem testifying in court about what their daddy did to their mama that night, and the many other nights they witnessed him pounding on her. Between the kids' testimonies, the EMS worker and pictures of Celeste's bruised body, it was an easy verdict. Whipper's arrogance didn't help much either. He said she wasn't a good wife and deserved every blow. It was a clear case of temporary insanity on her part, according to the judge. Time already served and probation made Celeste a free woman. Whipper, on the other hand, got ten years behind bars.

The wounds healed, but her spirit was broken almost beyond repair. That's when she met Jesus. One of the jurors ministered to her when the trial ended. Compassion goes a long way, you know. Juror number three happened to be one of our deacons. She visited Celeste a few times—just to be supportive and tell her about the Domestic Violence ministry we have here. Those short visits made a difference. Deacon-juror number three opened up the scriptures and introduced Celeste to Christ. It didn't take much convincing her that Jesus was the way to healing and salvation. She accepted Christ as Lord and Savior right there in her home—earnestly, with a sincere, repentant and forgiving heart.

"*Mother Jean,*' she told me. '*You should have seen the bucket of tears I cried just knowing that Jesus would heal my wounded soul. I can't say I forgave Whipper in that moment, but I forgave myself for allowing him to beat on me. And I forgave myself for allowing my children to be exposed to violence in my home. I even forgave myself for trying to kill that man the way he tried to kill me. It took a long time to find forgiveness in my heart for him, but eventually I did. He was a sick man and died in jail in his sickness. One day, he stepped up to the wrong inmate and lost his life. I'm sorry about that, but vengeance is mine, saith the Lord.*"

"*Love,*' she said, kept her there in the first place. They started out good—in love and loving life—always finding a reason to celebrate. The signs of domestic violence were there—verbal abuse and control. She just didn't want to believe he would hurt her."

"When did the DV start?" I asked.

"*Child number three,*' she told me. Number one was an absolute joy: a son—the pride of his loins. Child number two was his delight: a girl—his eternal admirer. He hit Celeste once or twice then because she didn't stop the baby from crying while he was watching television. Yep, child number three seemed to bring out the ugly in him. Maybe he couldn't take the pressure. That's when the beatings became regular. Then Whipper forced himself on her after a beat-down . . . and numbers four and five were conceived—the twins. After that, all hell broke loose."

I couldn't help but wonder, so I asked. "Why'd she continue to take it? Why didn't she leave after that?"

"She took it because he said he loved her; and if he didn't beat her, she wouldn't know that he loved her. Then he said he hated her—so he beat her because he hated her. She said she stayed because she needed him to love her again. Then he said he hated himself, and he beat her because he hated who he had become. That just made it worse because then she believed that he needed her; and with five children and no job, where could she go? What could she do? In her eyes, she needed him, too."

"She didn't tell anyone?" It hurt me to know that I already knew the answer.

"She said she wanted to, but knew he'd beat on her even more. That beast said he'd kill her if she told anyone, and she believed him. Said she knew that if she opened her mouth, she was dead. Then what would happen to her children?"

I shook my head. "That's so sad."

"Two years have come and gone since the spaghetti episode. Doesn't she look good! She's a Domestic Violence counselor now—no surprise. Still crying buckets of tears; tears of joy, and saving women's lives and leading them to Christ."

"She sure has a right to celebrate," I declared while watching Celeste hold on to the pew in front of her and stepping in place as if she were stomping on the devil's head.

Mother Jean shrugged her shoulders. "I'm just saying, son, after being liberated from all that abuse, who wouldn't give God His due praise?"

CHAPTER 5

Jasmine

(Super Storm Sandy)

❧

Mother Jean stretched her arms and shook her hands as if to increase circulation.

"I get a little stiff now and then," she said. "Do you remember Super Storm Sandy?"

"I do," I replied. "It was one of the worst storms I've ever seen. Fortunately, I live inland."

"Well, you were blessed. What I saw from the aftermath, I couldn't believe it myself! I tell you, the sea rose and covered the land. Rivers of water flowed through the streets like it did during hurricane Katrina down in New Orleans seven years before. Hundreds—thousands were left homeless. Until this day, people are still recovering from their loss.

Sandy came through with a fury and devastated entire communities. No one thought the meteorologists were right when they said the sea surge would be the problem. Evacuation signs were posted everywhere, and warnings were heard all over the news; yet, who knew it would be so bad. When Sandy finished her visit, it looked like a war zone around here--devastating.

This sister here, she pointed to a dark-skinned woman wearing a white dress with purple flowers. "Jasmine lived in the Rockaways. The way she tells it, the Atlantic Ocean and the Bay met on her doorstep and swallowed the house whole. When the water receded, a boat was parked upside-down in the driveway. Had she not gotten out when she did, no telling if she'd be alive to tell the story.

FEMA and the Red Cross helped so many people for months on end. Thank God for them and everyone else that flooded the Rockaways to help. I'm talking about humanity at its best. Good Samaritans came from all over the country with an abundance of food, clothing and supplies. But so many people lost so much; it just wasn't enough.

Relief stations run by local agencies were set up to help Sandy victims to fill out papers for emergency case management and housing. Jasmine worked for one of those agencies. I can't imagine how difficult it was for her to help the homeless when she, herself, was now homeless, too."

"It must have been difficult helping others when she was in the same situation," I declared.

"It's like that sometimes. More than you know," Mother replied. "It was something to see. Never in my life could I have imagined something like this. You know, you hear about natural disasters in other countries, and other cities, but never in New York. How I see it, Katrina's sister, Sandy, came to town and over-stayed her welcome!

Anyway, that's when I met Jasmine. She's such a nice girl. Some volunteers from the Redeemer got together and passed out blankets, food and water. Jasmine patiently waited her turn in line. I could see the distress in her eyes as she neared our table.

"What am I going to do? I lost everything?' She told me as I handed her a blanket. *'Everything I owned was in my basement apartment. Now it's all gone. My treasures are gone. They said it was an illegal apartment, so there's nothing they can do."*

"All I could do was express how sorry I was for her loss, but I knew she would get through this. Then I offered her prayer.

"If you think it will help," she reluctantly replied.

"*Oh yes,'* I told her. '*Prayer always helps. God will make a way for you if you believe. I know He will. I've never been through what you're going through right now, but prayer helped me during many hard times.*' I could see the hopelessness in her eyes. But she agreed and told me that she had nothing to lose since she had already lost it all."

"I know what it's like to lose everything," I interjected. Mother Jean gave me a look of inquiry; and then to my surprise, she began to pray.

"*Dear Father, help this young lady to see your good works even in this bad situation. You promised to take care of us . . . to be with us and to supply our every need. So I'm asking you to be with her and to supply her needs. Give her strength and courage to make it through this terrible crisis. I know you can and will bless her with more than what she lost. Do it for her, in the name of Jesus. Amen.'* I don't remember the exact words, but it went something like that."

"No doubt, your prayer meant a lot to her," I commented—thinking that it just meant a lot me.

"I believe so," Mother Jean replied. "Anyway, Jasmine parked herself on a folding chair under the FEMA tent and stared into space. I watched her half smile again turn blank with hopelessness. Then a tall man sat next to her and grabbed her hand. No telling what he said, but she looked at him in a way that made me cringe. She got up and walked away leaving her bag and blanket. It didn't look right to me. So I asked the security guard standing near my table to check it out. Sure enough, that man was up to no good. He was telling women that he could put them up for the night in a nice hotel. All they had to do was—well, I don't want to say, but you get the idea."

"He was on the prowl."

"That's right—a real predator!"

"It makes me sick to my stomach."

"Well, the security guard called the police. They escorted the man away in handcuffs. Sexual harassment, Jasmine later told me. She pressed charges to get him off the streets preying on more vulnerable young girls and women. Some other victims came forward, and helped to put him away for a while."

"That's good! Maybe he was a victim of abuse, too, and was acting out something that happened to him as a kid."

"Maybe."

"So what happened with Jasmine? I mean, look at her. She's really enjoying her praise!"

"She has a right to, son." Mother tapped my hand. "Long story short, she stayed in a shelter for a few months and found a nice apartment away from the beach—and not in the basement.

Jasmine received so many donations that she had to give most of it away. One Sunday, she came to church and testified about the *'lady under the tent who prayed'* for her. She wanted me to know that she survived Super Storm Sandy and was doing just fine.

She's a missionary now! Her heart is so warm and giving, and she keeps coming up with ways to help people in need. The entire homeless ministry was created by her—and no one comes in and leaves without being helped. You'd like her. Maybe after service, I'll introduce you."

"Mother Jean! So you're a match maker, too." I could feel myself blushing.

She smiled and patted the back of my hand, "I'm just saying."

CHAPTER 6

Mother Sharmaine

(Lester's Love)

❦

I discreetly looked at my watch. We talked for what seemed like hours, yet only forty-five minutes had passed. The music came to a slow halt, and the service Officiant thanked the worship team for the splendid ushering in of the Holy Spirit. I felt elated, even though my perch was a wooden folding chair in the basement Overflow Room.

Mother Jean shared with me so many wonderful stories about the sisters celebrating triumph over tragedies. Now I was ready to hear a good Word from the Lord and make my way home. Yet, I was pulled in by the intrigue of hearing another story. I vicariously lived each one of these sisters' testimonies through the elaboration of Mother's renditions of their *rendezvous* with the Holy Spirit.

"Now this sister here," Mother extended her hand and pointed to a mature woman with silver hair adorned by a white hat with purple silk flowers. "She was married to the same man for thirty years. A good husband, he was."

"Was?"

"Was," she continued. "Thirty years and three children—all grown now—and the most unexpected events started to happen."

"Like what?" I glanced at the screen and saw the ushers passing the offering plate. I pulled out my wallet and handed Mother Jean twenty dollars. "Mother, this is for the offering."

I didn't mean for her to go right then; but before I could call her back, she went up the stairs. As quickly as she disappeared, she reappeared.

"The choir will sing a few songs, and the guest preacher will come. I still didn't see any available seats. Praise the Lord, the house is full! You're stuck with me, son."

The couple that joined us earlier had already left. They said they didn't want to stay downstairs; and since there was no room in the sanctuary, they decided to make their way to another church. Me, on the other hand, I was intrigued by the wonderful third-party testimonies Mother told. I'd never seen these sisters before, and yet I felt as though I knew them personally. Something about each one of their stories touched a place in my own experience. It's amazing how connected we are as a people. Even with our many differences, somehow, our experiences collide.

"That's Mother Sharmaine," Mother Jean continued. "She and her Lester married young. He was nineteen, and she was eighteen. The perfect couple, they were. She became a teacher in the public schools; and he, an architect. They were in church just about every Sunday— didn't miss too many weekday activities either. Not even when the babies came along. Years went by, and Mother Sharmaine said things seemed different. She didn't know what it was, but definitely different."

"How so?" I asked.

"Well, she said she started noticing that her Lester wasn't so affectionate anymore. She thought after so many years of marriage, it was natural. *'It's normal,'* she told me. *'Couples go through these things— you know, the thrill is gone, but then it comes back again.'* I told her I understood because my husband once told me, *'Baby, the thrill is gone!*

It left on the Midnight Train to Georgia, made a U-turn and came on back to New York."

I had to laugh. "Never have I heard anything like that, Mother."

"He was a cad, my ole man. Anyway, you can imagine how she must have felt—not so good, to say the least. Then she chalked it up to mid-life crisis. Man-o-pause!"

"Men do go through a change just like women, only different," I interjected. "Did he start working out and always have something to do—somewhere to go?"

"Sure did. He stayed the gym when he wasn't working. Said he was making new friends. Said he had a lot of work to do at the job that kept him out late, too. Then he had conferences during the week and weekends—all business, so he said."

"And she believed him?"

"Of course, she believed him. There was no reason not to. Everybody believed him."

"Oh boy. I hear it coming."

"Yup! Mother Sharmaine started coming to church alone. Said her Lester was really busy—always too busy if you ask me. Said she didn't mind, though. The kids were old enough to go to church on their own if they wanted to; and with Lester's changing attitude towards her, she enjoyed worshipping without him lurking around with disdain."

"He would have brought her spirit down," I said empathetically.

"Umm hmm. One morning, he was packing his suitcase to go on one of those weekend business trips. That's when he told her he wasn't coming back home."

"What? Just like that?"

"Just like that. Then the truth came out. That ole Lester said he was gay. Said he'd been gay for years—like that Brokeback Mountain movie—only, she was too blind to see what was right in front of her.

Mother Sharmaine told me her mouth dropped open, and no words touched her lips. She was dumbfounded."

"That had to be devastating! After all those years of marriage, too. Wow!"

"The secret wasn't a secret, though. People were talking long before he told on himself. There were rumors, but no one had proof. Anyway, Lester said his lover was a business partner. They were at one of those conferences and shared a room like they always did. The way Mother Sharmaine tells it, he was sleeping when he felt a hand touch his legs under the cover. The thing is, he didn't reject the advance. Deep down he wanted to know why he felt strange sensations every time they were in the same room together; every time their eyes met, the unspoken was spoken. Then it happened and kept happening. He said they were in love."

"I can't imagine how that broke her heart."

"Ole Lester moved out; and two years later, Mother Sharmaine finally divorced him. The children stopped talking to their father for what he did to their mother; and they stopped talking to their mother until she cut him loose. To tell you the truth, if it wasn't for the children convincing her that their father was never coming back home, I think she would have held on until death—just like the wedding vow says."

"So what happened to him?" I had to know.

"He died. Not from the monster; not from AIDS. A massive heart attack took him."

I shook my head with an expression of sadness. "I'm so sorry to hear that."

"Don't be," Mother retorted. "Mother Sharmaine said it was the best thing that could have happened. Somehow, his death freed her from years of feeling that she was at fault for his decision to be with a man instead of his wife of thirty years. Said she was no longer tormented by nightmares of what she thought she did wrong; that caused him to go on the *'DL—down low.'* Said she buried her guilt and shame right along with his casket. You saw her getting her dance on. There's nothing like feeling free when you finally realize that it wasn't you. Shoot—I'll put an 'Amen' on that myself."

I must have looked at her strange because she raised her eyebrows and shrugged her shoulders as if to say, "What?"

"I tell you something else. God works in mysterious ways. Weeks before that heart attack, Mother Sharmaine prepared a family dinner. Said she couldn't take it anymore—her children not talking to their father, and she feeling like a failure. Said she invited everybody—the kids, Lester, and his partner, too. Getting them together like that was a miracle. Mother Sharmaine said, *'Forgiveness'* and *'Reconciliation'* sat down at that dinner table right along with them, and there wasn't a dry eye in the house. Now they have a special dinner on the anniversary of that day, and Lester's partner comes faithfully every year."

"Mother Jean, I'm beginning to hear a pattern. Someone died in almost every story you've told me."

Her eyes locked onto mine, "Death is a part of life, son."

"Don't I know it," I replied.

Mother Jean tapped her fingers on the table, bopped her head in sync with the offering music and stated as a matter-of-fact, "Most assuredly, God knows what He's doing, son."

CHAPTER 7

Melody

(Silent Worshipper)

J ust like Mother Jean predicted, the choir assembled after the offering and bellowed out a familiar song.

"I know that song," I declared. "It's one of my favorites. The choir is really singing!" My spirit began to dance within me. My feet began to tap the floor, and a progression of praise exited my lips. *"Oh Lord, we praise you!*

"Get your praise on, son. Praise Him."

And so I did. I rose up off of that wooden chair and sang along— hands clapping, foot stomping—until I couldn't sing any more. My voice mellowed into a whisper. I was thinking about the stories Mother Jean shared—and my own. I thought about how each sister's testimony touched my own. "Oh Lord," I shouted. "I praise you."

My eyes refocused on the screen, and I saw a young woman standing in the pew. She was wearing a purple linen suit with a white scarf attached at the shoulder, and a purple Fedora hat. I noticed that her hands were raised, but she stood in a silent praise.

"What's her story, Mother Jean?" I inconspicuously wiped a tear from my eye, but I think she saw me.

"That's Melody. Her name suits her well. She's like melodies from heaven—a gentle spirited woman. She's quite the looker, too. Melody survived a brain tumor a few years ago. She's such a sweet girl to have gone through what she went through. Talk about headaches—they didn't seem to go away. Every time we talked, she'd say, *'Mother Jean, I have a headache.'* I told her to go to the doctor time after time, but she didn't. Then one day, the pain was like fire, and she finally went to Urgent Care. It's a good thing, too. That tumor made itself right at home."

"Oh my! She doesn't look like she's been sick a day in her life—never mind a brain tumor."

"It's true. The doctors went to work on her right away. As soon as we got the news, the saints went to praying and praising God in advance for her healing."

"Praise God."

"Umm hmm. Praise God indeed! I tell you, we started a prayer call and prayed continually for hours. Bless God. Members responded like EMS responds to 911. Long story short, we prayed right through the surgery."

"What about her family? Where was her family?"

"Now that's another story," Mother declared.

I looked at her puzzled.

"The Redeemer Church is her family. Well, she has a sister, too."

"I don't understand. Please explain."

"Her parents died in a house fire."

I gasped.

"She and her sister were away at summer camp when it happened. The blaze was so fierce and spread so quickly, there was no escaping its deadly fury. What's so crazy is that it was the girls' first time at a sleep-away camp. They were supposed to return home the day of the fire. Oddly enough, the bus broke down, and they had to stay at camp another night. They would have been in the fire, too, if it wasn't for that broken down bus."

"Oh my goodness!"

"God watched out for those little girls. They were only nine and ten."

"Is there any other family?" I had to know.

"Somewhere in Europe, I'm told. No one stepped up on their behalf, so they were considered orphaned. The State put them in foster care, and that's where they grew up until they became of age."

"I grew up in a foster home," I revealed.

"Well then you know what it's like."

"I do. My parents were good to me. Not like some of the horror stories I've heard about from other foster kids, or in the news. They make a bad name for a good system."

"That's good." Mother took my hand and smiled. "Melody and her sister were moved from home to home. Said she'd never felt stable until The Redeemer became her place of refuge."

"What about her sister? Where is she?

"New Jersey. Gail is married with two children of her own. She comes to visit from time to time."

"At least she's not alone. She has Gail and her church. That's nice." I watched Melody extend her arms towards the ceiling and raise her head back as if she were looking into heaven. My heart felt an unexpected wave of compassion. I wanted to meet her and share stories about living in the system. I wanted her to know that someone understood what she went through. I wanted to comfort her if she needed comforting. Perhaps I was the one who needed to be comforted. I pondered. Perhaps Melody's story was *my* comfort.

"Son," Mother spoke softly to refocus my attention on her words. "She's alright. See how she's praising our God. Some might say she's a silent worshipper—but a worshipper, nevertheless. God does all things well."

I lifted my arms up high and quietly waved my hands. In that moment, I, too, became a *silent worshipper*.

CHAPTER 8

Mother Jean

(Victim to Victor)

∽

"What about you, Mother Jean? You've told me all about these celebrating sisters, but what's your story?"

"My story?" She looked surprised.

"Yes, Mother. What's your testimony?"

"Well, I hadn't thought about it much, but I suppose I could dig deep into my memory banks and pull out one or two."

"I'm sure you've got plenty!" We both laughed knowing that I was right.

"Well, okay. I was a victim of low self-esteem. Most of my early days in school were filled with bullying. I was overweight and didn't have much hair; and the hair I had was full of naps. Back then, most girls sat near the stove, and their mamas pressed their hair straight. Not mine. She said she wasn't going to burn out what God grew in. So I took my nappy, brushed-back hair head to school every day."

"Sounds like you had a rough time."

"I did! Life for me was really tough. I remember how the boys would pluck the back of my head for fun and call me 'Nappy.' The girls were even worse. 'Here comes Fatty-Nappy,' they'd say."

"That's so cruel. Did you tell your parents?"

"What was the point? It wouldn't have changed anything."

"Maybe."

"Nope. Once, I told my mother the kids were picking on me, and she told me to open my mouth and tell them where to go. Well, I did and got into a fight. That's when I learned I had to fight my way through life—literally."

"You were a fighter? That's hard to believe." I had to laugh because there's no way this regal woman sitting in front of me was ever a fighter.

"Believe it, son." She leaned back and observed the screen. "They're introducing the guest preacher."

I came to hear the Word, but now I wanted to hear Mother's story.

"The more they bullied me, the more I fought. Wound up in the principal's office so many times that my parents stopped coming to conferences and told the teachers they were weak because they didn't know how to handle me."

"You were a real handful!"

"I sure was. My nappy hair was no longer the issue. I grew out of that stage, and my girl curves took shape. The thing is, by my teen years, I became the bully—constantly provoking fights to prove myself. Juvenile detention claimed me for a year after my fists of fury landed that ole Selma in the hospital." Mother Jean balled up her fists and chuckled.

"You put someone in the hospital? She must have been pretty badly injured."

"Bloodied up—that's all. The scary thing is, if I had a knife or stick or metal pipe, she'd be disfigured—maybe dead."

"I'm scared of you," I said jokingly.

"See, the thing is, God knows what we need. Juvy-D saved my life."

"How so?"

"That's where I had my personal *rendezvous* with the Holy Spirit. That's where I met Jesus."

"What happened?" I leaned in and looked at the screen at the same time to see a mature woman grace the pulpit. Her purple and white robe was perfect for the occasion.

"The Redeemer Church conducted services every month to entertain us. At least that's what I called it—entertainment. All that singing and tambourine playing was getting on my last nerve, but it was a way to escape the monotonous routine of Juvy-D. My father was my only visitor—and that wasn't too often. Mother said she had enough of my shenanigans, and I deserved to be locked up for a while."

It seemed to me that her head slightly lowered as she recalled the troubled time.

"I was so depressed living in that jail for teens. I thought I was tough, but then the real bullies emerged. It felt to me just like my kid days of Fatty-Nappy. Once again, I became a target, and my esteem dropped to nothing. Needless to say, that's when I tried to take my own life."

"Did you really, Mother?"

"Yes, I did. I faked a bad stomachache and went to the infirmary. That's where I got my hands on them pills when the nurse stepped out of the room. That night, I took every one of them pills. I don't know how many I swallowed, or what they were. All I know is that I woke up in the same hospital where Selma was taken after I jacked her up."

"They pumped your stomach?"

"That's right. Oh, how my body ached when I came through."

"Who found you?"

"A guard found me laid out on the bathroom floor. Said I went in around midnight and never came out."

"They saved your life."

"They sure did. I guess God wasn't ready for me yet because that same week, The Redeemer Church came to entertain us." She laughed.

"Those young people sang their hearts out. For some reason, though, it felt like they were singing directly to me."

'Why are they singing to me,' I asked the girl next to me. She shoved me and said, *'No one's singing to you. Shut up.'* But I knew they were. Those young people kept singing—*Changed, I'm so glad He changed me.*"

"I love that song."

"I tell you, something happened down inside of me that I couldn't shake. Oh how the tears rolled down my face. I was clapping and crying and crying and clapping. Some woman came over and hugged me. Lord knows she wasn't supposed to do that, but she did—and I cried in her arms. Whimpered like a baby. She asked me if I wanted to know Jesus in my heart, and I said, *'Yes.'* Ever since that day, I've been following Him like a child follows after her daddy." She pointed her finger towards the ceiling signifying the "Him" of creation.

"Wow, Mother Jean. Your testimony is the cherry on top of a mountain of ice cream!"

She raised her hands in the air and shouted, "Glory! *I'm so glad He changed me.*"

CHAPTER 9

In Sync

(With the Holy Spirit)

❧

My heart filled with joy from hearing Mother Jean's recollection of these six sisters' testimonies—and her own. I could barely contain my excitement. I wanted to shout praises from the top of my lungs for what the Lord had done for them. I wanted to give God the highest praise—*Hallelujah*—for what I knew He'd done for me.

I gazed upon the screen as the guest preacher congratulated the sisters on their Women's Day celebration. She commented on how lovely they all looked in their purple and white combinations; how they displayed the royal beauty of holiness, and I wholeheartedly agreed.

"Mother Jean," I said. "I'm so glad to be here today. My intent was to come in, sit in the back pew and listen. I had no idea I was going to meet you and hear these wonderful testimonies."

"He's a wonder, you know. His plans always supersede ours," she declared.

"Can we see if there's a seat upstairs? If there isn't, I'll stand. I really want to be in the sanctuary to hear the Word."

"Of course, we can. There's no better place to be when the Word is going forth than where you can feel the heat of the Holy Ghost fire!" Her gentle laugh made me laugh, too. "I think you know just what I'm talking about, son."

39

"Yes, yes I do, Mother. I know there's a Word for me. I can feel it in my bones."

"That's good, son. The Lord's been speaking to you all along. You gobbled up the appetizer, and now it's time for the main course."

We ascended up the stairs and entered the sanctuary. Lo and behold, there was an empty seat in the third pew—right on the end.

"Looks to me like your prayers were answered," Mother leaned in and whispered. "Eat up, now!"

Before I could sit comfortably, she was already standing at her post in the rear sanctuary. My eyes gazed on the preacher, and my ears locked on to her every word. It was as though she was speaking directly to me—as if she had heard the many conversations Mother Jean and I shared in the Overflow Room. How did she know what was in my mind and in my heart? How could she have known the real reason why I came to church—the burdens of my heart?

"Everyone in here has had a personal encounter with the almighty God. You, you, you and you," she pointed in multiple directions. "And me, too." She pointed to herself.

"Amen," the congregation responded—as did I.

"Today, we've come together to celebrate what the Lord has done for each one of us sisters, personally. Oh, how our lives have been touched by the Master's hands. Aren't you glad about it?"

"Yes!" Shouts filled the room. "Amen."

"Then tell the Father, Thank You!"

A praise of, "Thank you, Jesus" erupted. My own praise collided with those of the congregation.

"Now I know many of you know I'm 'Old School.' You know how I do!" She leaned on the podium. "I'm gonna tell you like it is—straight up, with a Holy Ghost chaser! You came to celebrate Women's Day, I know; but what you really came to do is party hard for Jesus. Isn't that right?"

"Amen." Laughter echoed across the room.

"Look at how my sisters were dancing before the Lord like Miriam showing off your royalty in purple and white splendor; and, my brothers—so classy with your purple bow ties. You all have been dancing since I walked in the door. That's a good thing. After all, you came to the 'meeting place' to meet Jesus. You all are praising God in here as if you really know Him. It's a Holy Ghost *rendezvous* up in here! Somebody say, *'Rendezvous.'*

"Rendezvous," I shouted loudly along with everyone else.

"Beloved, this is God's appointed time and place. He called you here for a special meet-up; on this special occasion just to speak with you, personally.

Make no mistake about it, God called you by name and told you to come to church today because He planned this Holy Ghost rendezvous just for you. That's right. You thought you were coming to see what was going on in your neighborhood church. But God said, 'Come and go with me to my Father's house—the house of the Lord—so that I can talk to you. He pulled you away from your circumstances and plopped you front and center in the midst of praise just to talk to you. It's the praise that drew you, and the celebration of the God's Spirit that ignited the fire within you!"

I could feel my heart beating fast. I sure said to myself earlier in the morning that I was going to stop in the church and see what's going on . . . just because.

"When you got here,' the preacher continued, 'the Lord pulled you aside—in your spirit—and started the conversation. What you heard amazed you." She looked around the room. "Just like the book of Acts tells us about the day of Pentecost when the disciples waited in the Upper

Room for the arrival of the one Jesus described as 'the Comforter.' They went to the meeting place in Jerusalem as instructed—praying, singing and celebrating the resurrected Savior. He kept His promise, and now they waited on the arrival of another promise.

The anticipation of it all—knowing; yet not knowing, who this Comforter was, or how He would present Himself. All they had was their belief in a promise. Isn't that all you have today—a belief in a promise? God promised He would meet with you and talk with you, so you came to the one place you believed He would be; the place where you know He lives, the church. I tell you a truth. Today, He can live in your heart if you let Him. He will enter in and dwell within. Oh glory! Hallelujah!"

The whole church shouted, "Hallelujah," including me. Hands raised high!

"Oh, I know God is talking to someone today! In the middle of all the praise going on around you . . . in the middle of the Holy Ghost cheers; God called your name, and you responded, 'Yes Lord, here am I.' You came to get closer to Him. Well, I'm here to tell you that today is your day. Oh, praise our God. Today *is* your day! Whoever you are, God is speaking to your spirit, not your emotions. Everything you need is in Him. Everything you're looking for is in Him. Everything you've asked for is in Him. You came to this Holy Ghost *rendezvous* to have a personal encounter with Him, and you will not leave disappointed. God said, 'Now.' Come now—whoever you are, come now."

I thought she was staring directly at me when she made the plea, but her eyes were closed. My spirit instinctually heeded the call. It was as though I had no choice. I was compelled to 'Come.' So, I did.

An eruption of praise filled the sanctuary when I stepped into the aisle and walked forward. It was like a whirlwind from there. A tall thin man came from across the aisle and shook my hand. He talked as he walked me to the front of the church. All I heard was, "God bless you, brother. God bless you." He turned me towards the congregation, and I saw a sea of figures clothed in purple and white dancing in the aisles, the pews and near the back entrance.

The preacher came down from the pulpit and warmly embraced me. I felt the tears swell up in my eyes. Uncontrollable sobbing followed. Mother Jean made her way to the front and held me tight.

"Son, I knew the Lord was talking to you. Whatever it is, it's alright now."

I could hear the choir singing a familiar song—the same one as when I walked in through the church doors. Words from my own mouth erupted, "Thank you, Jesus."

My heart palpitated. My lips quivered, and I could hear myself speaking words I didn't know—that unknown tongue I'd spoken many years ago when I first received the Holy Ghost. That heavenly language when God spoke to me personally in a conversation that only He and my spirit understood.

When I came to my self, I knew that the Holy Spirit and I had had a divine encounter. I was surrounded by smiling faces. Mother Jean took the microphone from a nearby stand and began to speak.

"This here is Brother Russell. He hung out with me today in the Overflow Room. Come on and show him some love."

Applause and shouts of *"Hallelujah"* went up to the heavens. I stood there with my arms open wide to receive whatever else the Lord had for me. My eyes were blurry from tears, but I could see the six sisters I'd come to know through Mother Jean's stories. There was Glenda, Ramona, Celeste, Jasmine, Mother Sharmaine and Melody—all smiling and clapping or waving their hands in praise.

The preacher put her hand on my shoulder and spoke in a whisper.

"So you're the reason I'm here today. You're the prodigal son the Father is calling home."

"Home? Where is home?" I thought. Suddenly, I realized that it wasn't the church building. Home is where my Father is, in my heart—in my spirit. God had called me to be reconciled with Him in my heart and spirit. I *was* Home.

"Is there something you'd like to share?" The preacher asked. "Go ahead, tell your story."

The tall thin man that ushered me to the altar handed me a paper towel. I wiped my face and shook my head in amazement. I took the microphone into my hand and slowly began to speak.

"It's been a long time since I've been in church," I confessed. "A few weeks ago, I lost my foster mother to cancer. She's the only mother I knew. I held her hand as she slipped away. Her last words were, *'Son, find your way back to the Lord.'* My heart was really heavy this morning, and I thought maybe I'll come inside the church instead of walking by like I've done so many other Sundays."

"Praise Jesus," the preacher said looking up towards the heavens.

"The first person I met was Mother Jean. She kept me company downstairs and shared the testimonies about some of the sisters here. Each story unexpectedly touched a place in my own life. Each one was my own story in some way."

I felt the tears begin to flow again. Mother Jean rested her hand on my back as if to give me support.

"My mom would always say, *'Son, home is where your heart is.'* My heart is with the Lord," I declared. "Father, I'm home. Thank you, Jesus."

Praise exploded in the sanctuary—as did the crescendo of music and angelic voices of the choir. I kneeled and bowed in surrender to worship my God—thanking Him for this divine *rendezvous* with His Holy Spirit.

"Look at God," the preacher bellowed. "Come on church. Get your praise on!"

And the celebration continues . . .

Rendezvous: The Journal

❧

There's a time and place when God arranges a divine *rendezvous* to get our attention. It might be in the middle of a snowstorm, a natural disaster, a life-changing tragedy, an eye-opening experience, or a betrayed relationship. Then again, it might be during a joyous event and celebration like the one Russell experienced during a Women's Day service.

Without introduction, the host arrives and quietly peruses through the crowd observing, listening, smiling, laughing, assessing, facilitating connections and putting out small embers of impatience and inquiry with a single word. Finally, someone notices that this unassuming guest is the center of the event, and He has engaged us all.

What about your own divinely orchestrated Holy Ghost meet-up? Do you remember when and where you met Him—God? Do you remember when "knowing about Him" led to "knowing Him"? Did you recognize when the Holy Spirit arrived in your circumstances? Did you rally around Him with anticipation of what was going to happen next? Did you understand that all things were working together for your good regardless of the situation?

"Rendezvous: The Journal" invites you to reflect on your own life-changing experiences. Each of the 25 journal topics has three sections: God is; Prayer of thanksgiving; and, Prayer of intercession. I encourage you to take your time and be present (show up); be real and honest with yourself; and, pray and allow the Holy Spirit to lead you.

Enjoy the journey.

Abundant blessings
Rev. Michele Jackson Taylor

1.

Healing

(From illness, physical affliction, emotional duress and depression)

God is my Healer:

_____

_____

_____

_____

_____

_____

Prayer of thanksgiving for my healing:

_____

_____

_____

_____

_____

_____

Prayer of intercession for healing others:

_____

_____

_____

_____

_____

_____

2.

Comfort

(In times of grief, loss and sorrow)

God is my Comforter:

_____

_____

_____

_____

_____

_____

Prayer of thanksgiving for being my comforter:

_____

_____

_____

_____

_____

_____

Prayer of intercession that God would comfort others:

_____

_____

_____

_____

_____

_____

3.

Deliverance

(From domestic violence, abuse, neglect or maltreatment)

God is my Deliverer:

_____

_____

_____

_____

_____

_____

Prayer of thanksgiving for my deliverance:

_____

_____

_____

_____

_____

_____

Prayer of intercession that God will deliver others:

_____

_____

_____

_____

_____

4.

Provisions

(When unthinkable and unpreventable disasters happen)

God is my Provider:

_____
_____
_____
_____
_____
_____

Prayer of thanksgiving for being my provider:

_____
_____
_____
_____
_____

Prayer of intercession for providing for others:

_____
_____
_____
_____
_____

5.

Compassionate Companion

(When I feel unloved, unwanted, rejected, abandoned and betrayed)

God is my Compassionate Companion:

_____
_____
_____
_____
_____
_____

Prayer of thanksgiving for being my compassionate companion:

_____
_____
_____
_____
_____
_____

Prayer of intercession for being a compassionate companion to others:

_____
_____
_____
_____
_____
_____

6.

Strength

(When I feel overwhelmed, lost and alone)

God is my Strength:

_____

_____

_____

_____

_____

_____

Prayer of thanksgiving for strengthening me:

_____

_____

_____

_____

_____

Prayer of intercession for strengthening others:

_____

_____

_____

_____

_____

7.

Victorious Warrior

(Victory over bullies, low self-esteem and self-harm)

God is my Victorious Warrior:

_____
_____
_____
_____
_____
_____

Prayer of thanksgiving for giving me victory:

_____
_____
_____
_____
_____

Prayer of intercession for the victory you're giving to others:

_____
_____
_____
_____
_____

8.

Restoration

(He restores my soul)

God is my Restoration:

_____
_____
_____
_____
_____
_____

Prayer of thanksgiving for my restoration:

_____
_____
_____
_____
_____

Prayer of intercession for restoring others:

_____
_____
_____
_____
_____

9.

Liberation

(Freedom from stress, anxiety and worry)

God is my Liberator:

_____

_____

_____

_____

_____

_____

Prayer of thanksgiving for my freedom:

_____

_____

_____

_____

_____

Prayer of intercession for the freedom you're giving others:

_____

_____

_____

_____

_____

10.

Protection

(Against the hands of the enemy)

God is my Protector:

_____
_____
_____
_____
_____
_____

Prayer of thanksgiving for your protection:

_____
_____
_____
_____
_____

Prayer of intercession for your protection of others:

_____
_____
_____
_____
_____

11.

Shelter

(From dangers seen and unseen)

God is my Shelter:

_____

_____

_____

_____

_____

_____

Prayer of thanksgiving for being my shelter:

_____

_____

_____

_____

_____

_____

Prayer of intercession for being a shelter for others:

_____

_____

_____

_____

_____

_____

12.

Covered

(Your banner over me is love)

God is my Covering:

_____
_____
_____
_____
_____
_____

Prayer of thanksgiving for covering me:

_____
_____
_____
_____
_____
_____

Prayer of intercession for covering others:

_____
_____
_____
_____
_____
_____

13.

Preservation

(Kept in my right mind and health)

God is my Preserver:

_____
_____
_____
_____
_____
_____

Prayer of thanksgiving for preserving my mind and body:

_____
_____
_____
_____
_____

Prayer of intercession for preserving the mind and body of others:

_____
_____
_____
_____
_____

14.

Shield and Buckler

(Repelling fiery darts and the powers and principalities of darkness)

God is my Shield and Buckler:

_____
_____
_____
_____
_____
_____

Prayer of thanksgiving for shielding me from the powers of darkness:

_____
_____
_____
_____
_____

Prayer of intercession for shielding others from the powers of darkness:

_____
_____
_____
_____
_____

15.

Rock and Fortress

(Standing on solid ground)

God is my Rock and my Fortress:

_____

_____

_____

_____

_____

_____

Prayer of thanksgiving for being my rock and my fortress:

_____

_____

_____

_____

_____

Prayer of intercession for being a rock and a fortress for others:

_____

_____

_____

_____

_____

16.

Guardian

(The guardian of my soul and spirit)

God is my Guardian:

_____
_____
_____
_____
_____
_____

Prayer of thanksgiving for being the guardian of my soul and spirit:

_____
_____
_____
_____
_____

Prayer of intercession for being the guardian of the souls and spirits of others:

_____
_____
_____
_____
_____

17.

Over-Flowing Joy

(Contentment beyond measure)

God is my Joy:

_____
_____
_____
_____
_____
_____

Prayer of thanksgiving for giving me over-flowing joy:

_____
_____
_____
_____
_____
_____

Prayer of intercession for giving over-flowing joy to others:

_____
_____
_____
_____
_____
_____

18.

Renewed Hope

(When all hope is gone)

God is my Hope:

_____
_____
_____
_____
_____
_____

Prayer of thanksgiving for renewing my hope:

_____
_____
_____
_____
_____
_____

Prayer of intercession for renewing hope in others:

_____
_____
_____
_____
_____
_____

19.

Ever-Lasting Peace

(The peace that goes beyond understanding)

God is my Peace:

_____
_____
_____
_____
_____
_____

Prayer of thanksgiving for giving me ever-lasting peace:

_____
_____
_____
_____
_____

Prayer of intercession for the everlasting-peace you give to others:

_____
_____
_____
_____
_____

20.

Faithful Friend

(The one who gave His life for His friends)

God is my Faithful Friend:

_____

_____

_____

_____

_____

_____

Prayer of thanksgiving for being my faithful friend:

_____

_____

_____

_____

_____

Prayer of intercession for being a faithful friend to others:

_____

_____

_____

_____

_____

21.

Shekinah Glory

(A divine Rendezvous with your Holy Spirit)

God is my Shekinah Glory:

_____

_____

_____

_____

_____

_____

Prayer of thanksgiving for my Rendezvous with your Shekinah Glory:

_____

_____

_____

_____

_____

Prayer of intercession for the Rendezvous others will have with your Shekinah Glory:

_____

_____

_____

_____

_____

22.

_____

God is my _____:

_____
_____
_____
_____
_____
_____

Prayer of thanksgiving for _____:

_____
_____
_____
_____
_____

Prayer of intercession for _____:

_____
_____
_____
_____
_____

23.

God is my _____ :

_____
_____
_____
_____
_____
_____

Prayer of thanksgiving for _____ :

_____
_____
_____
_____
_____
_____

Prayer of intercession for _____ :

_____
_____
_____
_____
_____
_____

24.

_____

God is my _____ :

_____
_____
_____
_____
_____
_____

Prayer of thanksgiving for _____ :

_____
_____
_____
_____
_____
_____

Prayer of intercession for _____ :

_____
_____
_____
_____
_____
_____

25.

_____

God is my _____:

_____
_____
_____
_____
_____
_____

Prayer of thanksgiving for _____:

_____
_____
_____
_____
_____
_____

Prayer of intercession for _____:

_____
_____
_____
_____
_____
_____

ABOUT THE AUTHOR

Author Michele Jackson Taylor (a.k.a. Rev. Michele) has over 30 years of leadership experience in the Pentecostal church including: administration, dean of Christian education, assistant pastor, pastoral care, and ministry consultant. Her literary works are inspired by what she's experienced and learned during her faith walk and span over such genre as religious/inspirational fiction, non-fiction and romance. Publications include: "The Making of You," "Blackberry's Wine," "The MJ Collection," and "In Loving Memory."

Rev. Michele is the Founder/Executive Director of Comfort and Joy Ministries, Incorporated—a faith-based nonprofit organization whose mission is to promote the Gospel of Jesus Christ through the ministry of service and soul care. She is a member of the New York State Chaplain Task Force (NYSCTF), and the American Association of Christian Counselors (AACC).

Rev. Michele holds a Master's Degree in Social Policy from the State University of New York Empire State College; a Bachelor's Degree in Sociology (with a focus on the Sociology of Religion) from the College of New Rochelle/School of New Resources; a Certificate in Ministry from New York Theological Seminary, and various Certificates of Completion from courses taken with the American Association of Christian Counselors. She is currently a doctoral candidate at Northwestern Theological Seminary.

Rev. Michele resides in Brooklyn, New York, and enjoys being a servant of the Most High God.

Printed in the United States
By Bookmasters